What I Wore

What I Wore

FOUR SEASONS, ONE CLOSET, ENDLESS RECIPES FOR PERSONAL STYLE

Jessica Quirk

BALLANTINE BOOKS TRADE PAPERBACKS
NEW YORK

A Ballantine Books Trade Paperback Original

Published in the United States by Ballantine Books, an imprint of The Random House
Publishing Group, a division of Random House, Inc., New York.

Library of Congress Cataloging-in-Publication Data
Quirk, Jessica.
What I wore : four seasons, one closet, endless recipes for personal style / Jessica Quirk
p. cm.
ISBN: 978-0-345-52610-6—ISBN 978-0-440-42366-9 (ebook)
1. Clothing and dress. 2. Fashion. 3. Beauty, Personal. 4. Seasons. I. Title
TT507.Q64 2011
746.9'2—dc22   2011001438

Printed in the United States of America

www.ballantinebooks.com

0 9 8 7 6 5 4 3 2 1

Book design by Liz Cosgrove

For my parents, Dan and Linda Schroeder, who taught me to draw as soon as I could hold a crayon, who never teased me for changing my clothes at least twice a day, and who sent me to New York City to follow my dreams

Contents

Introduction

A COOKBOOK FOR YOUR CLOSET

One day in eleventh-grade art class, I looked up at a poster on the wall listing practical art-based careers such as architect, graphic designer, and museum curator. Of all of them, I remember being especially interested in fashion designer—and thinking that was right up my alley but probably something that could never happen for a girl born and raised in Indiana.

Flash forward to my sophomore year at Indiana University. After two semesters of standard prerequisites, I yearned for a more creative outlet and switched from business to an apparel merchandising major, and also applied to get on track for the costume construction technology degree. In these classes, I learned how to sew, draft patterns, and make gloves, hats, ballet tutus, and corsets, as well as how to draw fashion illustrations and put together a design portfolio. Instead of spending time at the library, I was in the sewing lab, chatting away with my peers about how we'd one day make it to New York City (and most of us did!).

Then, the summer before my senior year, I was accepted for an internship with legendary New York fashion designer Betsey Johnson. As much as I learned in school, I learned even more when I set foot into her Manhattan office. And every night, while living in an all-girls dorm on West 34th Street, I would dream up my own imaginary collections—sketching, coloring, pulling together palettes and swatches, and preparing for the day I'd become a fashion designer in my own right.

After graduation, I spent the next four years working my way up the ladder as an assistant, then associate, then head designer for a small company that did private labels for big mass merchants. Private labels are in-house brands that are often manufacturered by multiple companies.

The production aspect of the fashion industry is highly segmented for the greatest possible productivity. Our specialty was bottoms: skirts, shorts, and jeans. Another company would do T-shirts and another company would make jackets. For my job I traveled all over the world—from London to Paris for research and inspiration, to Hong Kong and China to develop samples.

And it was in Hong Kong, on an average afternoon, that I stumbled into the world of daily style bloggers—women of all ages, sizes, and income levels were taking photos of their outfits every day. At the time, my wardrobe was nothing to write home about, but I liked what I saw and thought I might try it myself.

And I did! I took and posted my first daily outfit photo on May 5, 2007, and haven't stopped snapping away since. Then I started my blog—What I Wore—and eventually left my design job to pursue blogging full time. By documenting each outfit, along with the when, where, and why that accompanies each look, I've been challenged to keep things fresh, evolve my personal style, and work with what I already have in my closet.

My foodie parents proudly gifted me cookbooks, nonstick pans, and stainless-steel pots when I graduated from college. I guess they were hoping I'd take on some of their culinary magic. I grew up in a household that rarely ate out (meaning a home-cooked hot dinner was on the table *every* night), and I can promise you there are at least two hundred cookbooks lining the shelves in my parents' den. Not only do my parents love good food, but after years and years of practice they've become masters in the kitchen. My husband is the same way—he's the kind of guy who opens an empty refrigerator and ends up throwing together the best meal I've ever eaten.

After all these years, I've realized that getting dressed is a lot like cooking. Just like an expert chef in his kitchen, a chic woman is able to open her closet doors and put together a perfectly styled outfit with ease. She knows the best places to shop, what textures and patterns work well together, and how much sass to add to an outfit (and when adding too much totally spoils the look).

What am I getting at here? I'm not so naturally gifted in the kitchen. I've never been able to *whip something up*. It's just not my thing. But I *can* follow a recipe. So when I try something once, twice, three times, it ends up tasting pretty good.

When I set out to write this book, I thought a lot about how cookbooks are organized and formulated. It crossed my mind that even really good cooks (*hello Mom and Dad!*) continue to push themselves to experiment with new recipes, constantly taking cuisine to another level. Once you think you're good at something, be it a recipe or pulling together an outfit, it's time to add another dimension to the whole thing. It could be experimenting with a new flavor profile at the dinner table or introducing an item of clothing in a bold new pattern.

Like cooking, you don't need to be born with an innate sense of what goes with what to be a really stylish gal; you just need to figure out what works for you. The great thing about a cookbook is that it's the *starting point*. My goal with *What I Wore: Four Seasons, One Closet, Endless Recipes for Personal Style* is to help you create your own twist on a basic recipe—to take stock of what's in your closet, help you with a shopping list, and cook up outfit after outfit that makes you feel great about your-self. I'll explain what pieces work year-round and which transition from season to season. I'll show you how to put together clothes for work out-fits, weekend outfits, and going out/evening outfits. And along the way I'll toss in handy little "*I never knew that*" tips to up the ante on your wardrobe and keep you in high style. From there, you can infuse your own person-alized variations on classic combinations.

As you flip through the book, you'll notice I used one faceless model body in a variety of skin tones and hairdos. I want *you* to image *yourself* in these outfits—to get ideas and take them in any direction you choose. And just as great chefs take classic recipes and give them a twist, I hope you do the same with your own clothing and your own closet.

What I Wore

Getting Started

TAKING STOCK OF WHAT YOU'VE GOT AND BUILDING A SMARTER CLOSET

Between my freshman and sophomore years in college, I took a summer job working in a factory that produced quilted handbags out of a small Midwestern town. *Perfect!*, I thought, here was my first foray into the fashion industry. I worked on the cutting line—pulling fabric from the bolt onto a long table and stacking it twenty or thirty layers deep in a seven-yard space. I worked with a partner and our favorite things to talk about were variations on *If I could only have twelve pieces of clothing, what would they be?* and *What would you buy with a bajillion dollars?* Since then, I've always kept a little running list in the back of my mind of what I'd do in either of those situations—how I could make the most of a closet limited to a dozen items versus what it would be like to completely make over my closet from scratch with a wad full of cash.

Let's talk about your *actual* budget. No matter how much money you have to spend per season, the questions are the same: What to buy? Where to spend? Where to save? For a four-season climate, your yearly budget should be roughly broken down to:

30 percent for spring (This is when you'll buy most of your warm-weather clothing.)

15 percent for summer (Add-on pieces like sundresses, skirts, and blouses in lighter-weight fabric—which also cost less.)

45 percent for fall (Spend now for the majority of your cold-weather clothing, including a coat, shoes, boots, denim, etc.)

10 percent for winter (Spruce things up with a few heavier sweaters and holiday items.)

KEY CONCEPTS

Basics: classic pieces in core colors that you wear year after year and that work for every season.

Core colors: neutral building blocks like black, dark brown, or charcoal gray

Secondary colors: bright or bold trendy colors that are season specific (for example, pastels in spring or jewel tones in fall)

Add-ons: trendy and seasonal pieces that round out your closet

Let's start with the basics and add-ons every woman should have in her closet.

Color Story

PICK YOUR CORE COLOR

When you're getting started with your year-round *basic clothing,* it's best to stick to a *core* color—like black, dark brown, or charcoal gray. A lot of women end up with nothing to wear because they've limited themselves to wearing an item only one way (this happens when you shop for head-to-toe "looks"). If everything in your closet flows from one piece to the next, from outfit to outfit, you're left with so many more potential combinations. That flow is best achieved by starting with the following basic items in one core color:

✓ CHECKLIST

- Blazer or jacket
- Cardigan
- Button-up blouse (in white or off-white)
- Camisole

- Trousers
- Little black dress
- Opaque tights
- Skirt
- Dark denim jeans

Once you feel your basics are covered in one core color (and you're buying quality, classic clothes that last more than a single season), expand into a new core color.

If you can afford to spend more on the basic part of your closet, do it, especially for investment pieces such as blazers, slacks, skirts, and coats. Although your head-to-toe look doesn't need to cost a fortune, wearing one high-quality (and sometimes more expensive) item can make your *entire* outfit look more polished. You can get away with spending less on tights, tees, and casual sweaters because these need to be replaced more often and are not usually the focal point of an outfit.

SECONDARY COLOR PALETTE

Next, start to add diversity and pattern into your closet with a new set of what I'm calling your *add-on* pieces. While your core colors work year-round, your seasonal add-on pieces will be in *secondary colors*. For this example, I've started with the blues and purples in the prints of the dress and skirt. From there, I've added on a violet cardigan that works with both pieces. For each new garment you add-on, make sure there's something it will work with in your current closet (basics or other add-on pieces). Key add-on pieces include:

✓ CHECKLIST

- Printed dress

- Solid dress in secondary color

- Printed skirt

- Solid skirt in secondary color

- Cardigan in secondary color

- Printed or solid blouse in secondary color

- Solid tanks in secondary colors

- Solid tights in secondary colors

I usually spend less money on items that are multicolored or patterned because they have less mix-and-match possibilities than their solid-color counterparts. And while you might wear the same bold-printed skirt two weeks in a row, you probably won't wear it two *days* in a row like you can with a solid-colored cardigan or skirt.

The idea here isn't to be matchy matchy with every single item you have—your closet doesn't need to look like a color-coordinated boutique. Instead, it's more about buying clothes that flow from one outfit to the next, like the tights and cardigans and accessories that transform your investment pieces into weeks and weeks worth of outfits.

> **PRO TIP:** When shopping, make a rule for yourself that each *new* piece you buy goes with at least three things you *already have* in your closet.

Shoes

Shoes may be a small part of your outfit, but they're an important one. The bulk of your shoe collection will be specific to your needs (standing all day, work safety, lots of walking), but don't limit yourself there. To be covered for almost every occasion, the most basic shoe stash should contain:

✔ CHECKLIST

- Black or brown high heels

- Black or brown flats

- Nude heels (because they work with *everything*)

- Black or brown boots (riding or heeled)

- Walkable flats (canvas sneakers, sandals, or slip-ons)

Of all these shoes, walkable flats are the pair that need to come with a warning: White gym sneakers should never, *ever* be worn with business suits, office outfits, or cocktail dresses (or really any place other than the gym). If you have a long walk to and from your job, go ahead and get a supportive pair of walking shoes, but spice things up by going with an old-school color palette (like burnt orange, maroon, mustard yellow, navy) or go with some funky flats with built-in cushioning.

In the following chapters I've paired up the shoes I think will look best with an outfit, but you can always swap out flats for heels or vice versa.

◉ The Foundation

Finally, buy yourself some decent underwear! Get rid of anything that doesn't make you feel good about your body (and you know exactly what I'm talking about). A modern woman might argue that slips are for grannies, but they'll make your clothes flow when you're wearing tights or hosiery. I've had luck finding them in specialty lingerie boutiques, finer department stores, and vintage shops. They've been a lifesaver so many times for me that I'm slowly but surely adding to my collection with different lengths and colors. And the proper length is important—just the other day I attempted to roll the waistband of a half slip so it didn't show under the mini-skirt I was wearing. Big mistake! Within half an hour the hem of that slip started to creep down to reveal itself. *Not cute.* Slips should always be *shorter* than your skirt.

For your foundation garments I recommend:

✓ CHECKLIST

- Seamless bra and undies to match your skin tone (these should be virtually invisible under all clothing)

- Seamless strapless bra to match your skin tone (invisible under all clothing and good for thin straps/strapless tops)

- Black seamless bra and undies (invisible under dark clothing)

- At least one set of matching bra and undies in a fun/sexy color

- Foundation shorts (for super-tight dresses and tummy control)

- Half slip (to wear under skirts)

- Full slip (to wear under sheer dresses)

◉ Analyze Your Closet

Now that you know what you need to buy to get your wardrobe into tip-top shape, let's figure out what you already have that's worth keeping. When I take stock of my closet, I remove everything from the shelves, drawers, and hangers and throw it all on my bed (so I can't talk myself out of the job and crash for a nap halfway through). This is the kind of project that takes a lot of energy, so you should plan for an entire Saturday or Sunday with a mind-set of determination. Once you have one giant pile, assess each piece and create three new piles: yes, maybe, and donate/resell. With each item you pick up, use your flash judgment. At the beginning of the process, you'll feel like putting a lot into the "yes" pile, but as you progress, you'll be getting rid of the pieces that don't make you look and feel your best. You might even want to go through the "yes" pile again and try to narrow it down even more. A lot of women hold on to clothes years after the last time they wore an item, telling themselves, "I might need this later!" The truth is, you probably *won't* need it later, and if you get rid of something you're not wearing anyway, you open the door to replace it with something that you'll love even more.

Now it's time to try everything on. It might sound crazy, but it's a waste of space to put things in your closet that don't fit, and it's aggravating when you reach for that piece when you're in a rush. Anything that's not within one size of fitting perfectly needs to go to the tailor or Goodwill. (I make one exception to this rule. On the back shelf of my closet I keep one pair of "skinny" jeans for when I'm feeling extra sexy and one pair of "slouchy" jeans for when I'm not.) Take everything that doesn't fit or is no longer to your taste and put it in another room so you're working only with the good stuff. While you're trying each item on and checking it out in a full-length mirror, ask yourself:

Does it flatter my body?

Did I feel great the last time I wore it?

Can I remember the last time I wore it?

If you answer no to any of these questions, get that item out of your closet, pronto.

The important thing to remember is to build your closet around the life you're living now. If you spend most of your time at the office, buy work clothes. If your primary interest is comfort, find ways to be practical yet stylish. If you love nightlife, buy yourself some sexy tops and dresses. It's all about balance to suit *you* and your time. I'll go into more detail on your basics, add-on pieces, shoes, and accessories for each of those situations in the following chapters.

◉ *In Your Closet or Store for the Season?*

Now that you have separated out the best of your wardrobe, everything should be clean and ironed before it goes onto a hanger and back into your closet. Just like clothes that don't fit, it doesn't make sense to have wrinkled pieces that put up a big ol' roadblock when you're already short on time. If you hate to iron, keep that in mind when you head out on your next shopping trip, and stop buying fabrics that get wrinkled easily. I find that most of the time, if you hang your clothes up right after they're washed and dried, you'll be fine. Otherwise, send anything that needs to be pressed to the cleaners if you can't bear to iron it yourself.

What about seasonal gear? Only keep out the current season's clothes and put everything else out of sight. Granted, you'll have crossover items that work from season to season (or even year-round) like jeans, button-ups, blazers, and basic dresses, but anything for extreme weather should be packed up. I have pretty small closets, so it's absolutely essential for me to pack away out-of-season clothing in space-saving bags, big plastic tubs, or in unused suitcases and store them out of sight. (For me that's the top and back of my closets, but dry attics and basements also do the trick.) I know so many women with closets that are packed to the brim who still always end up feeling like they have nothing to wear, which is true if you have sundresses hanging in your closet in winter or puffy coats in summer. So do yourself a favor and only work with the ingredients for the season and the weather outside your door.

⊙ Tools of the Trade

After the clothes and shoes and accessories, there are a few things every gal should also have on hand to take proper care of her wardrobe:

- **Cascade-style flocked hangers** to save space
- **Full-length mirror** near your closet
- **Ironing board** and **steam iron**
- **Lint roller**
- **Small sewing kit** containing scissors, safety pins, straight pins, black and white thread, small multicolor thread set
- **Jar for all those extra buttons** that you may never use but will be very happy to have in one place should you need them
- **Tape measure** for cross-checking measurements when online shopping
- **Shoe polish kit**

And if you're really into having fun with your closet and have the space:

- Folding clothing rack (great for packing and laying out/organizing a week's worth of outfits)
- Upright steamer
- Three-way mirror (always check your front *and* backside before dashing out of the house)
- Dress form to display scarves and bags (or even full outfits)
- Wig forms for hats (either very awesome or very creepy)

HANGERS FYI

Flocked hangers are covered in slip-free fabric to prevent your clothes from falling off

Wooden hangers are ideal for heavier items like jackets and coats or suits

Plastic hangers can work double duty for hanging slacks or blouses

Trouser Clip hangers are ideal for skirts or pants hung by the hem

Wire hangers aren't great for long-term use—they can easily snag clothing and leave permanent poke marks on the shoulders of your blouses. Toss 'em!

Always and Never

Although I'd like to believe there aren't a whole lot of rules left in fashion, there are some things I'd classify as "Always" and "Nevers." My fashion favorites and pet peeves:

ALWAYS

- Wear what flatters your body, regardless of the trends
- Remember, how you feel about yourself is the most important part of getting dressed
- Have a go-to outfit ready in your closet for mornings when you feel uninspired
- Find time to play dress-up and create new outfits (like on Sunday night with a glass of wine)

NEVER

- Wear pants with dragging hems
- Sport a muffin top
- Buy something just because it's on sale
- Wear flip-flops (except for the salon and the beach)
- Wear brown corduroy in summer, yellow chiffon in winter
- Leave the house in a dirty or wrinkled outfit
- Wear bunchie undies under body-conscious garments (or ever?)
- Resort to safety pins instead of a tailor (except in emergencies, of course)

So now you have a wardrobe that may be a bit smaller, but it's full of clothing that you love, that's clean and pressed, and that *fits*. You're off to an excellent start!

Spring

When people in New York find out I'm from Indiana, or people from Indiana learn I've moved to New York, they always ask me what the biggest difference is between the two. Usually they expect me to say something about the cost of living or how I see celebrities on a daily basis, but the reality is, I spend more time outside in New York. When you live in such small apartments (my first place was about the size of my parents' living room back home), you rely on your neighborhood to serve as your backyard and you spend a lot more time on foot to run your errands. I don't have a car, so my boots really do need to be made for walking, and yes, I'm probably going to change into higher heels when I get wherever I'm going. Everything I wear has to work both inside and out, and it's been a great challenge.

No matter where you live, there's no season that requires more creativity and flexibility with the weather than spring. Your closet will need to take you from snow to rain, from freezing to sunny and 60 degrees, and everything in between. With a little planning, you'll be the girl who's properly prepared and looking cute for a perfect storm, a chilly morning, or the first beautiful *real* day of spring.

In this chapter, we'll identify what winter clothes to keep in your closet, what to pack up and put into storage for next year, and what to add-on to keep your closet feeling fresh.

Spring: Pull from Your Closet

Depending on your climate, mid- to late March is a good time to transition over from your winter to spring wardrobe. First identify what winter basics like turtlenecks, tights, dark skirts, dresses, and jackets will work for layering. You'll want to pack away most of your dark colors and nubby sweaters (especially pieces with a holiday vibe).

In addition to all of your crossover pieces, unpack all of your bright skirts, dresses, and blouses from storage. Remember to try everything on, then launder and press before you put onto hangers and into your closet.

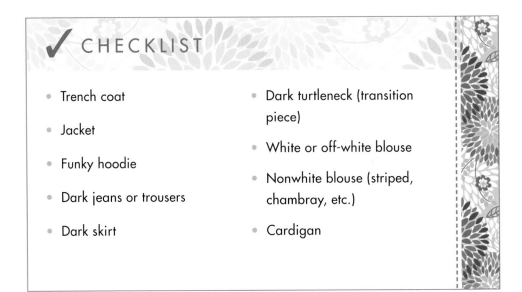

✔ CHECKLIST

- Trench coat
- Jacket
- Funky hoodie
- Dark jeans or trousers
- Dark skirt

- Dark turtleneck (transition piece)
- White or off-white blouse
- Nonwhite blouse (striped, chambray, etc.)
- Cardigan

◉ Spring: Add-Ons

Along with last year's wardrobe of prints and brights that made the cut from your most recent closet clean-out, it's always nice to add a few pieces in updated colors. I definitely *don't* advocate replacing everything with the new shade of the season, but adding in a few T-shirts or cardigans will rev up your entire spring wardrobe. I always see my old clothes in a new light when I bring a fresh piece to the table.

I've put together two secondary color palette examples for you—one with cool tones like blue, violet, and neon yellow, and another with richer, warmer hues. Remember to choose colors that not only work together but also look great with your skin and hair color. In general, go with tones that contrast your natural coloring. Gals with rosy complexions look great in shades of blue. Redheads look amazing in greens and turquoise. Yellow always looks pretty on a tan. Violet looks beautiful on almost every skin tone. The key with color is to not blend in with what you're wearing.

Also notice the stripes on the next page: Narrow vertical stripes are slimming and can make you look taller, while horizontal stripes can give the illusion of more width. If you're proportionally larger on the top half of your body, go with thin stripes. Women who have pear-shaped bodies or smaller chests can get away with wider stripes on top.

CHECKLIST

- Solid dress(es) in secondary colors

- Printed dress(es)

- Solid skirt in secondary color

- Printed skirt(s)

- Solid cardigan in a secondary color

- Solid blouse(s) in secondary colors

- Striped blouse(s) and tees

- Sweater

- Cropped jacket(s)

PRO TIP: A *pattern* is a design woven into the fabric. A *print* is a design printed on top of the fabric.

⊙ Spring Splurges

The first "designer" item I purchased in New York City was a pair of dark green, mid-heeled MARC by Marc Jacobs rain boots—and I've never looked back. It's been seven years since and I've racked up dozens of compliments and day after rainy day of use.

Depending on your climate, spring is a smart time to set aside some shopping money for a pair of well-crafted rubber rain boots. Spend extra now and you won't need to replace them for ten years or more.

Splurge with:

- Glossy mid-heel rain boots—chic and polished
- Black wellies—dress up or down and wear forever
- Ducks—decidedly casual, save for weekends

Don't forget your umbrella, either! For years I relied on cheapie deli/gas station $3 umbrellas and ended up windblown and soaking wet. Now I have a small collection of a variety of sizes and colors that I put a bit more money into (but not *that* much). There's something about a bright yellow or hot pink umbrella that makes bad weather less of a drag.

When you wake up to a rainstorm, the last thing you should do is dress to match the weather. Skip the monotone or all-black ensembles in favor of a little color to bring some pep to your step. I even like to push myself to coordinate an outfit around a particular color (neon yellow or hunter green) as an additional rainy-day challenge. Here are a few outfit ideas that can brighten up even the gloomiest day:

PRO TIP: When wearing your rain boots for your commute, make sure to bring along a pair of shoes to change into. The weight of the rubber can get really heavy by midday, and who knows if it'll be raining when you leave.

⊚ Spring Shoes

I always combine a mix of winter and summer shoes for spring in addition to my rain boots. If it's chilly, stick with close-toed boots, booties, or pumps. Once it's a bit warmer, bring out your clogs, wedges, and flats.

PRO TIP: If you're wearing a winter coat, you should be wearing winter shoes. Save your open-toed shoes for warmer days.

tall sandal

spring/summer nude
high-heel sandal

winter bootie

flat slippers

brogues

◉ Spring Accessories

Accessories are a great way to bridge the gap between seasons and add a bit of warmth or a splash of color. For example, the first few weeks of spring are pretty chilly, so I like to wear a cheery scarf with a black turtleneck and springlike skirt with tights. The difference between a winter and spring ensemble can be as simple as going for a light cotton scarf over a heavy knitted one. Big chunky necklaces are an inexpensive update and another quick fix for making your outfit feel seasonally forward.

vintage leather belt

cotton scarf

silk scarf

costume necklaces

watch

⊙ Storage: Jewelry

Jewelry storage is all about keeping things neat and tidy so you can find what you want, when you want it. That's why I hang my jewelry on nails on the inside of my closet. I've seen a lot of clever variations, and anything will work as long as necklaces are kept hanging (untangling two teeny tiny chains is my worst nightmare!).

For my smaller pieces, like broaches or earrings, I use clear craft store dividers and plop each piece into its own little section.

For bulkier pieces, like bracelets and bangles, I use clear plastic boxes and just pile them in.

◉ Spring Work Outfits—Week One

You've heard that old saying "in like a lion, out like a lamb," right? It always runs through my head when I'm getting dressed at the beginning of the spring season. Transitional elements like jackets, scarves, and tights bring the warmth factor to your outfit and still work well with springlike pieces. This week, let's look at some ways to extend your wardrobe into five unique looks using layering. Each ensemble utilizes the basic part of your closet, plus incorporates some of those new add-on pieces (and even some items from your winter closet).

A silk scarf tied around the neck and paired with a jean jacket has such a Parisian vibe and also covers your bases for being cozy on a chilly spring day. Pair with a Breton striped long-sleeve tee for even more of a French feel (Outfit 3).

If it's still a little too cold to wear a spring skirt with bare legs, layer it over thick tights, boots, and a turtleneck. The predominately black basic pieces let the new add-on skirt grab all the attention (Outfit 1).

⊕ Spring Work Outfits—Week Two

This workweek, take a look at outfits based around patterns, specifically stripes. They work for girls with a more conservative style and also for those with funkier vibes. Another reason stripes are great? They can be the star of the show or blend in as a neutral part of your outfit.

For example, in Outfits 1 and 5, a very fine stripe functions as a neutral and lets the other elements of the outfit stand out. Think of stripes in these two outfits as best supporting actors, while the green trench and black tights in Outfit 1 or the sequin sweater in Outfit 5 take the leading roles.

To make an instant statement, a larger, bold stripe, as in Outfit 4, adds just as much impact as the bright-colored skirt it's paired with.

⊙ Spring Work Outfits—Week Three

For our last workweek, it's all about pops of color. Some of my favorite outfits are the result of crazy color combinations that you might not initially think of. For example, I love this very simple navy-and-cream-striped top with dark trousers that's hit with a bold splash of color in the scarf and then paired with red shoes (Outfit 2).

I also love using a print against color, like with this leopard and coral combo (Outfit 3). The belt, jacket, and grounding black shoes keep it professional, but the color makes it really fun.

● Food for Thought: A Gal and Her Handbag

I'm a purse girl. I love handbags. I crafted my first little mini purse when I was ten years old out of an old dress and continued to sew bags for myself and my friends through college. I love them so much, in fact, that instead of posters, rows of purses adorned my college sorority bedroom walls. There's no denying that a great handbag can enhance any outfit.

Go with the highest-quality leather handbag you can afford that coordinates with the core color of your wardrobe (black, brown, or gray). I tend to go with bigger bags that will accommodate a laptop, a SLR camera, and a notebook, along with everything else that normally goes into a purse. Tally up what you lug around day to day and choose your bag size accordingly.

I like to add a handbag in a new color and shape every year. If you properly care for your bags, you'll be able to carry them for years and start a collection. Keep tabs on the state of your purse—once the thread on the handles starts to come undone or your bag is visibly dirty, it's time to either have it professionally mended and cleaned or take it out of your rotation for good.

For gals on a budget, I'd suggest a sturdy cotton canvas tote or vintage bag. I'm not a fan of cheap, flimsy pleather bags, but there are some quality, well-made styles available for those who would rather not carry leather. Pass on knockoffs as well—if you want a status bag, rein in some of your other spending and save up instead of going with a cheap phony. Cheap bags *look* cheap. End of story.

For evening events, downsize your pocketbook to a small clutch big enough to hold your cell phone, lip gloss, mirror, and credit card/cash. You'll want to choose something big enough not to bulge when full and will be comfortable under your arm or in your hand all night long. If you're more of the hands-free sort, opt for a style with a removable cross-body strap.

clutch

classic handbag

bucket bag

hand/shoulder bag

◉ Spring Weekend Outfits—Week One

For a lot of us, the weekend is our chance to show off our personal style. The last thing you should do is go from put-together-woman Monday through Friday to total slob on Saturday and Sunday.

Growing up in Indiana meant jeans, jeans, and more jeans for the weekend. People everywhere really love their denim (I do, too!), but the right print and cut of a skirt or dress can be just as casual for weekend wear. You want the effect to be more easy breezy than dressy, so look for cuts that aren't too tailored and are a little more on the flowy side. As for

fabric, opt for easy wash-and-wear cotton or linen and steer clear of material that's too fancy (satin, taffeta) or businessy (structured wool) for your weekend activities.

On the previous page are a couple of examples for cute weekend outfits based around a skirt and a dress. First, a short, watercolor-printed skirt is loads of fun with a striped tank top borrowed from summer and a lightweight cardigan (Outfit 3). Perfect for a picnic or springtime stroll. On the other hand, if it's still a bit cool outside, wear a very short dress *over* jeans and throw on a trench (Outfit 2).

> **PRO TIP:** When layering a dress over pants, make sure it's either a supershort variety or can be tucked and pinned to tunic length.

⊙ Spring Weekend Outfits—Week Two

This weekend, I'm going to take you through five different denim looks—everything from your basic blue jeans to head-to-toe denim. Speaking of . . .

> I just bought a new chambray shirt, but I'm not convinced wearing denim on denim can look good. It seems kind of cheesy and matchy matchy. Any ideas?
>
> —Sarah, 23, Georgia

Denim on denim—it can either be a Wild West mistake or ultrachic. To make the combination work well, choose denim with the same hue but of drastically different shades (imagine both were the same color initially and one piece was washed fifty times). For example, a lightweight, washed-out chambray button-up looks classic with darker jeans (Outfit 5). Whatever you do, avoid a matching-jacket-and-jeans tuxedo-like combo.

If you're opting for a more polished effect with your jeans, go for a dark shade—like navy (Outfit 2) or black (Outfit 3). I especially like dark denim because it can work well for so many occasions—for weekend looks as shown here, for casual Friday at the office, or with a glitzy top for girl's night out.

PRO TIP: Slim-fit skinny jeans should be hemmed at the ankle. Wider leg openings (like boot cut) should fall halfway between the top of your heel and the floor.

◉ Spring Weekend Outfits—Week Three

Can I wear white year-round? I live in a part of the country where it's pretty warm from March to November and it seems silly to limit my light closet to traditional summer months.
—Carolyn, 21, Florida

I'm sure you've heard those old edicts of fashion faux pas like no white before Memorial Day. I think wearing true white (unlike creamy winter white) is more of a climate thing than a calendar thing. Once you're get-

ting 80-degree days, you've got carte blanche to pull out those crisp spring and summer whites (Outfit 2).

Another white item that actually works year-round is a standard white button-up or any variation on a white blouse (Outfit 5). For this spring ensemble, a coral skirt and khaki trench coat make for a springlike look, even when paired with practical winter boots.

PRO TIP: Skip white shoes with a white dress—it looks too ceremonial/bridal. Instead, opt for nude or cognac brown shoes (black looks too harsh) for a leg-lengthening look.

⊙ *Food for Thought: Say Yes to Vintage!*

When I was a little girl, I went through a "pioneer" phase while reading the *Little House* and *American Girl* books. This meant, naturally, that I needed to dress head to toe like a little prairie girl. We're talking calico cotton dresses, petticoats, bloomers, thick black tights, and lace-up boots (apron, bonnet, and braids optional). Thinking back on it now, this was the beginning of my interest in costume history and, subsequently, vintage clothing.

Fast forward a decade to my first year in New York City with a slim budget. Vintage and thrifted clothing were the only way to get the look I was going for, and I've been wearing secondhand duds ever since. Wearing vintage clothing is sustainable, chic, and often at bargain-bin prices (although high-quality, well-curated vintage can be quite expensive).

So what makes something vintage? Or thrifted? Or an antique? How can you tell what era a garment is from? Here's a quick breakdown for buying vintage clothing.

- *Thrifted* clothing means it was purchased secondhand.
- *Vintage* clothing is at least twenty or more years old.
- *Antique* clothing is generally no longer wearable and for display only.

The key to buying vintage is the same as bringing any new piece to your closet: Does it work with what you already have? Could you pair that fifties skirt with a modern blouse? What about that boxy sixties jacket with skinny jeans and booties? If it makes sense, buy it, love it, and keep it forever!

Characteristic Details from the 1950s to the 1980s

1950s

Natural waist

Full skirts

Cardigan suits

Tailored blouses

1960s

Boxy jackets and coats

Dress/jacket sets

Miniskirts and dresses

Mod look

Graphic and op art prints

1970s

Prairie dresses

Empire-waist dresses

High-waisted jeans and trousers

Crochet

Disco dresses

Wide collar points

Polyester

1980s

Exaggerated shoulders

Acid wash

Secretary blouses

Tea-length, high-waisted skirts

Color blocking

Every time I go to a thrift store I feel both overwhelmed (so much stuff) and underwhelmed (I can never find anything that great). Do you have any tips on how to make thrifting a better experience?
—Jennifer, 32, Nebraska

Going to a secondhand or thrift store can be a great adventure. If you're lucky, you live in a town with a clean, well-priced store. Maybe you're *really* lucky (like me) and have a store that carefully curates the merchandise. Either way, here are some tips to help you break into the thrifting world with as little discouragement as possible.

1. Ignore the size tag—vintage clothing is marked much larger than its modern cousins. In most secondhand stores, return policies are nonexistent. Try everything on—not just to make sure the item fits right (like sizes, vintage cuts are different), but also to better check for flaws like stains or holes that you might not see on the hanger. Don't bet on anything coming out in the wash and buy anything damaged with caution. Speaking of the wash, always take your secondhand pieces straight to the laundry room before you hang them alongside your current closet—there's no guarantee the item was laundered before it was dropped off.

2. Start small . . . literally. Most thrift stores have bins of old poly and silk scarves. Chances are good you'll find a piece or two here, giving yourself the confidence to move forward.

3. Coats. Look for classic styles like trench coats and peacoats. Trends in outerwear don't cycle over as quickly as regular clothing, meaning you'll be able to buy a gently-used style and still look completely modern.

4. Shoes. Some of my favorite pairs have come from the thrift store, but I've also just gotten too excited and bought other pairs that didn't end up fitting comfortably. Buy your day-in, day-out shoes at a store you equate with comfort and style and leave your thrifted shoes for fun. If they end up being a pain, at least you didn't spend much on them.

5. Dresses and skirts. This area has a lot of potential. I love those old disco dresses from the seventies and secretary dresses from the eighties (especially if there's an elastic waist that allows for flexibility in sizing). Always look for the overall potential of the item! Dresses and skirts that are too long can easily be hemmed to look very modern.

6. Blouses/tops. Silk secretary blouses and cotton band T-shirts are generally your best bet. As with dresses or skirts, some alterations may be necessary.

And for the daring . . .

7. Pants. If you're going to buy pants secondhand, you need to be patient and full of energy to hit the fitting room. The cut of jeans and slacks has *really* changed a lot over the past few decades and you might find yourself faced with tons of full-thighed, tapered acid-washed jeans (elastic waist anyone?). First sift through for color or wash and then narrow down to modern silhouettes—and always try them on!

◉ Spring Evening Outfits

There are no hard-and-fast rules on what to wear for a fun night out; it really all depends on who you're with and, more important, where you're going. When I'm home in Indiana, playing pool and listening to a live band, I'll pull together an outfit that's really low-key, like jeans and a cute top. On the other hand, for a New York City girl's night out, you'll find me in something a little dressier and more fun. No matter where I'm going, or what I think other people will be wearing, I always remember what my Mom told me when I was younger: *It's better to be a little overdressed than a little underdressed.*

Nighttime lets us push the limits—a little more shine, higher heels, and shorter hemline (just not all at the same time).

On the opposite page are five evening outfits that span the gamut. Try a glittery cardigan with a barely there camisole and a short black skirt for a flirty date or a Saturday night out with the girls (Outfit 1). If you're headed to a pool hall or dive bar, dress up black jeans and a blue chambray blouse with a sparkly necklace and a pair of spring heels (Outfit 3).

⊛ Style Challenge: The T-Shirt

Outside of the gym, I'm not a huge fan of freebie/event T-shirts (so much so that I cut up all of my college tees and made them into a quilt upon graduation). However, they seem to be the dress code for casual Fridays or over the weekend, and truthfully, they can look pretty cute. Whether you amass them from supporting a favorite team, your kids, or from a charity event, make sure you're wearing the correct size (nothing three sizes too big) and try the following outfit combinations.

For a downtown look, pair your favorite cutoffs with black tights and booties and throw on a smart black blazer. Roll up the sleeves for an even cooler feel. Next, if you're the kind of lady who can't get enough of skirts, try pairing your tee with a full, watch-me-spin skirt, a fun costume necklace, and a vintage belt. Finally, go behind your basic jeans-and-tee vibe by donning dark skinny jeans, high boots, and a scarf for a rocker chic ensemble.

T-shirt

Summer

CHIC, SWEAT-PROOF SOLUTIONS
FOR WORK OR PLAY

There's something baked into American culture that makes summer feel like the most carefree season of all. Maybe it's that we spend our childhood straitlaced and in tidy rows while school is in session and then run like little wild animals from the school bus as it drops us off after the last day of class. (Oh man, I really loved that day! Such potential! Such freedom! A whole summer ahead at the pool, playing capture the flag, campfires, and family vacation!)

I think the free feeling of summer sticks with us through adulthood. Most corporate culture lightens up between Memorial Day and Labor Day with alternative dress codes for staying cool. And just as when we were kids, summer is still the season of bike rides, days at the beach, outdoor concerts, and picnics galore.

In this chapter, I'll guide you through promotion-worthy office looks, superchic weekend outfits, and great going-out ensembles. And if you've ever been stumped about summer wedding dress codes or what to wear to the company picnic, fear not. What about the right bra for skinny straps or how to pack a suitcase? I've got you covered.

Chill out . . . and let's get dressed for summer!

Summer: Pull from Your Closet

You've already pulled all of your lighter-weight clothing out of storage for your spring closet, so many of your warm-weather wardrobe pieces were introduced then. Once you hit early June, add the following into your rotation:

✓ CHECKLIST

- White layering tank/camisole
- White skirt
- White dress
- White jacket or blazer
- Dark summer dress
- Dark summer-weight trousers (linen, cotton, or tropical wool)
- Summer denim (a little more beat up/washed or white denim)
- Dark cropped cigarette pants

◉ Summer: Add-Ons

Of all the seasons, your summer add-ons will likely be the least expensive—summer items use less and lighter-weight fabrics—allowing you room in your budget for experimentation. However, this is a season when you don't need to buy tons of new pieces. Instead, add a few new sundresses each year along with loads of *color*! Another seasonal bonus? Summer staples—like nautical/sailor looks or red-white-navy color palettes—pop up again and again, keeping those small summer purchases in style year after year.

✓ CHECKLIST

- Tees and tanks (solid or printed)

- Printed blouse(s)

- Tunic or caftan (solid or printed)

- Solid blouse in secondary color

- Solid cardigan in secondary color

- Printed or solid dress

- Printed or solid skirt

- Romper

- Funky jacket

- Summer sweater

⊙ Summer Splurge: Your Bathing Suit

If there's one thing you should spend a little bit more summer money on, it's your bathing suit, especially if you have a pool membership, a beach rental, or a vacation planned in the summer months. There are definitely options available in all price points, but I opt to spend a bit more on a suit I can add to my collection rather than wear for only one summer. Spending a bit more cash can also make you feel worlds more comfortable than swimwear that doesn't offer the proper support or coverage. Get something that makes you feel great about your body! There are push-up tops, tummy-control slimmers, and cute boy-cut shorts that are *totally worth it*.

retro two piece   one piece   string bikini

PRO TIP: Because bathing suits are seasonal merchandise, retailers will need to clear them out starting mid-July to make room for fall collections, which means big sales and major savings!

Summer Shoes

Like summer clothing, shoes in the summertime are often at a lower price point than during other seasons. You'll carry over a lot of styles from spring, so only add-on where necessary. My go-to pair are strappy bronze flats (metallic shoes work with just about any outfit), but I also suggest nude high-heeled sandals, work-to-weekend black wedges, wood and leather clogs, canvas slip-ons or sneakers, espadrilles, and fun flat sandals in a pop color.

metallic wedge

nude high-heeled sandal

flat sandals
(metallic and pop color)

espadrille

black wedge sandal

wood and leather clog

I can't talk about summer footwear without bringing up rubber flip-flops. While I don't mind them at the beach, by the pool, or at the salon, they look sloppy with an outfit that was put together with a lot of thought. You wouldn't trade in your handbag for a plastic grocery bag or use an envelope instead of a wallet, so don't downgrade your ensemble by finishing it off with messy footwear.

PRO TIP: Getting used to new sandals can bring on dreadful beginning-of-the-season blisters! Always carry a dozen heavy-duty bandages in your purse and an extra pair of sandals or slippers that can easily fit into the bottom of your handbag.

⊚ Summer Accessories

When it's too hot to layer sweaters and jackets, turn to accessories to complete your look. In addition to fun jewelry, summer-weight scarves are practical for when you want to be prepared for the weather to get a bit cooler at night, or when you'll be spending time indoors in air-conditioning. Straw accessories, like hats or belts, are a great way to "summerize" some of your early-spring outfits, too. Finally, don't forget sunglasses! I like to buy a new pair each summer, which is a great way to build a collection.

gauzey summer scarf

vintage silk scarves

straw belt

elastic and metal-closure belt

straw fedora

necklace
(can be worn as a belt)

sunglasses

⊛ *Food for Thought: How to Wear a Summer Scarf*

Summer scarves are a simple, easy way to add a little extra spice to your outfit. They're also pretty cheap and easy to find from secondhand shops, street vendors, or department stores. Vintage scarves in particular are a great source of color inspiration and can effortlessly pull together colors you'd never thought of. (I love the navy, lavender, and red combination shown on the opposite page.)

Here are a couple of different ways to incorporate scarves into your summer wardrobes:

1. Cowgirl tie. Use a large square scarf folded along the diagonal. Tie a double knot at the nape of your neck, allowing the scarf to fall loosely.

2. Half turban. This little mock turban has retro pinup flare. Start with a long rectangular scarf or a large square folded in on itself from the diagonal. Rest the center of the scarf at the nape of your neck and wrap to the front of your hairline. Cross the scarf over itself twice (to create a little raised loop), and twist back to the starting point and tie in a double knot. This looks especially cute with a high, messy bun.

3. Hat band. Tying your scarf around a hat gives it a fresh and coordinated look. Use a long, thin scarf or a folded square and wind around the base of the hat. Tie ends in a double knot, tucking any extra length under the band. Dress it up even more by pinning a vintage brooch (or two!) at the knot.

4. Secretary. A simple necktie is so sophisticated and French! This option works for scarves of any shape or size. I like to pop the knot over to the side and off my shoulder.

Let's make getting ready for work in the summer as easy as possible. I'm breaking down summer office ensembles into three sections: outfits for temperatures in the 70s, the 80s, and on those killer 90-degree days. First up, the cooler side of summer.

⊙ Summer Work Outfits—Week One, 70 Degrees

Don't shy away from long sleeves just because it's summertime! Breezy tunics or colorful cardigans in summer colors and fabrics are great options for cooler days. Coral is such a pretty summer color, too, and looks really great with navy. Try a flirty playful outfit by tucking a striped tank top into a full navy skirt with a coral cardigan and contrasting belt (Outfit 2). For a relaxed but pulled together vibe, wear the cardigan with a matching striped tee and pair with easy dark trousers (Outfit 5).

⊙ Summer Work Outfits—Week Two, 80 Degrees

Here are five outfit ideas for warmer days that can get up into the 80s. Most workplaces don't allow bare shoulders (read: spaghetti straps) in their dress codes, but that doesn't mean you need to look or feel dowdy when it's hot out (or feel limited to a basic black cardigan to cover up). Partner up short-sleeve and sleeveless tops with an office-ready jacket to not only look professional but feel comfortable in that chilly AC.

A year-round basic black blazer works perfectly with a ruffled animal-print blouse and khaki skirt (Outfit 1). When you're layering, remember that there's a chance you're going to remove your jacket or sweater, so make sure your blouse or top is appropriate.

Another favorite recipe of mine is pairing together contrasting dresses and jackets. For example, a sophisticated summer dress looks so chic with a lightweight jacket (Outfit 4) (drop the jacket and you're ready for a weeknight dinner date on the town).

◉ Summer Work Outfits—Week Three, 90 Degrees

The biggest summer wardrobe challenge of them all? Balmy, sticky weather that takes the temperature into the 90s. Translate your weekend "stay cool" strategy into the workweek with lightweight, natural fabrics like cotton and linen. Opt for silhouettes that flow away from the body, instead of a super-tailored fit.

I like to always focus on accessories on hot, humid days, because even a super-simple eyelet blouse and black skirt (Outfit 5) can really come together with a great belt and the right jewelry. A word of caution here: When pairing a white top with a black bottom, there's always a risk of

looking like a caterer. Stay safe by picking a blouse other than a basic button-up, or add sophisticated touches of color through a belt or neck-lace.

Another stay-cool strategy is to wear a lightweight dress for your com-mute and add-on a colorful neck scarf once you've cooled off and gotten settled at your desk (Outfit 2). The little touches like the scarf and belt makes a breezy, simple outfit a professionally polished one.

⊙ Food for Thought: Bra Straps

Girls, let's talk about bra straps. Once summer hits and those tank tops and spaghetti straps come out, you're going to have to think twice about what bra you choose to wear:

1. Strapless bras are the best bet if you can find one that's com-fortable enough to wear for extended periods of time. I've never been a huge fan, but I recently found a great style that's seamless and has plenty of built-in support (look for styles with clear "sticky" gel that keeps the bra from sliding down). Because your goal is to hide this bra completely, go with a color that matches your skin tone.

2. If you're wearing a racer-back tank, wear a racer-back bra. If you don't want to fork over the cash for something you don't think you'll wear that much, check out the "as seen on TV" section of your local drugstore for clips that transform a regular style into a racer back.

3. The back band of your bra should never be hiked up so far that it's visible—that's a sign you're wearing a bra that's way too small to be supportive. Go have a bra fitting!

4. Now, if you're going to let your straps show, make sure your bra is a style with thin, pretty straps. A color that matches your top will look so much cuter and show a little forethought with your outfit. I like buying fun, colorful bras for just this reason.

5. Halters, tube tops, and one-shoulder tops will never look great with a normal bra. If you are uncomfortable with a strapless or convertible style, just skip these kinds of tops!

summer strap no-no   cute and coordinated

Summer Weekend Outfits—Week One

When I think of summer Saturdays and Sundays, my mind floods with picnics, barbecues, beach days, and a lot of socializing. Sure, you could lounge around in the same old pair of cutoffs or jeans, but why not put in a tiny bit of effort and grab a compliment or two on your summer style? During this time of year, my outfit inspiration starts with fun, bright colors.

Violet blue contrasts beautifully with any skin tone, making it a sure thing for everyone in the summertime. For Outfit 2, I paired summer camp-style blue shorts with an Indian embroidered tunic. A straw hat and bold summer scarf pull everything together and just look so dang *cool*.

Another one of my favorite summer outfit tricks is to take a button-up blouse from your work closet (or even borrow one from your husband or boyfriend) and tie up the tails. Paired with a full and swingy skirt, it looks straight out of *Roman Holiday* (Outfit 3).

◉ Summer Weekend Outfits—Week Two

When I think of layering, it usually has to do with staying warm, but when done well it can also be a great way to transform an outfit in the summer. For example, get more wear from a summer romper by layering it with a full dark skirt (Outfit 1).

Or on cooler nights, throw on a basic, beat-up jean jacket. Like jeans, a faded denim jacket goes with almost everything in your closet (except light to medium blue) and looks so fresh with a full white skirt and straw belt (Outfit 2).

◉ Summer Weekend Outfits—Week Three

I've suggested a couple of outfits based around this full white skirt and straw belt combo (Outfit 2). Such super summery pieces can transform even a vintage black-printed blouse into a laid-back-looking outfit. Throw on a straw hat and flat sandals for a perfect park outfit or add heels and glam sunglasses for a chic al fresco dinner date.

PRO TIP: Pass on buying white bras and undies, even in the summer. Not only do they show through with white and pale-colored garments, but they can catch a camera flash underneath darks. You're better off matching to your outfit or going with a flesh-tone set.

⊙ Style Challenge: Summer Wedding

Summer is *the* season for weddings, so here's a quick decoder on appropriate wedding attire. First and foremost, never wear anything that might upstage the bride or call undue extra attention to yourself. This means no white (unless the bride has requested it), no extra flashy colors or prints (good-bye, neon yellow!) or skimpy cuts.

A wedding's dress code should be indicated on the invitation, but if it's not, look for the time and location of the ceremony and reception as a clue. In the past, almost all weddings were religious and formal affairs. Times have changed and you'll probably be a guest to a slew of different kinds of weddings. Also keep in mind:

- **Formal and black-tie weddings** (after seven o'clock in the evening) indicate that the gentleman should be wearing either a suit or a tuxedo and women should dress accordingly. Fancy cocktail dresses or gowns are appropriate.
- **Semi-formal weddings** are usually held in the evening (five o'clock or later). Cocktail or tea-length dresses are your best bet.
- **Garden weddings** are morning or early-afternoon affairs (before five o'clock). Floral-print dresses are appropriate, as well as nice linen or cotton in a demure color. The cut of your dress should be a bit more conservative than for an evening wedding.
- **Weddings held on a beach** are often informal, so opt for a dress that works barefoot and will stay put on a windy day.

Here are a few more tips on deciphering what works and what doesn't for the summer wedding season:

- For weddings before five o'clock in the afternoon, skip black. If you must wear a dark color, opt for navy.
- The fabric of your dress can make or break your entire outfit. Save the heavy velvets, taffetas, and brocades for winter months. Summer dresses should be in polished cotton, silk, or polyester.
- If you are absolutely dead set against wearing a dress, a dressy suit with an evening blouse and cocktail jewelry will be appropriate.

black tie   formal/evening   semi-formal/
                                           evening   garden or daytime   beach wedding

- For any wedding ceremony held in a place of worship, you should cover your shoulders with a shawl or scarf and research any additional formalities.
- Don't forget that your hair, makeup, and jewelry can transform a simple dress into the perfect outfit. An up-do and flashy jewelry can make a day dress a little more elegant for the evening, and softer hair and makeup appear more casual.

More likely than not, you know the bride or groom, so just use your best judgment. Just don't be that one wacky cousin in head-to-toe tangerine popping into the background of every photo.

◉ Style Challenge: Company Picnic

Let's say your office is throwing an off-site summer morale booster or team-building picnic and the forecast is 92 degrees and humid—you won't be expected to don the same head-to-toe look as your everyday dress code, but what *can* you wear? First and foremost, no matter the location, the other attendees are still your co-workers (and your superiors and assistants), so don't wear the same kind of outfit you'd wear to a picnic with your girlfriends.

If your HR team doesn't send out a memo, it's safe to say you can go one step more casual than your normal nine-to-five wardrobe. For example, if you wear business attire all week, a short-sleeve blouse and less tailored cotton jersey skirt will be perfect (Outfit 3). Or make some of your work-week pieces a bit more laid back by untucking or tieing up the tails of your shirt (Outfit 2). If you wear jeans to work, shorts (but not too short!) and a T-shirt are suitable. As for shoes . . . aim for something comfortable (no five-inch heels, please) and appropriate to the venue. You'll want to pass entirely on beat-up gym sneakers and beach flip-flops.

Summer Evening Outfits

For nine months of the year I recommend limiting your exposed skin to just one area for going out at night. But in the summer, it's OK to show off more because of the heat. The line between tasteful and trashy rides on how you go about showing that skin . . . and your shoes. A teeny tiny dress with flat shoes looks a lot more tasteful than a teeny tiny dress with five-inch heels (Outfit 2). Just remember, the shorter your hem is, the flatter your footwear should be.

⊙ Food for Thought: Packing a Suitcase

Could you give advice on what essential clothing items a stylish woman should pack with her for a summer vacation? I'm a terrible packer and I want to get the most out of wardrobe options without packing a ton of clothes. Thanks.

—Rebecca, 34, Tennessee

Planning is the most important part of packing a suitcase and feeling great about your clothes on a trip or vacation. Start your process by identifying your major clothing needs—for a business trip that might mean a suit; for a wedding, a cocktail dress. For vacation you'll need comfortable walking shoes. Before you get too ahead of yourself, also check the weather forecast for wherever you're headed and, when in doubt, bring layers. I like to start by hanging together (or placing together in piles on the bed) individual outfits and then *trying them on.* It's worth the effort to find out before you leave that (a) something doesn't fit, (b) there's a stain, or (c) you just don't like the outfit that much. Once you have two or three full outfits, work with the various components of each to create additional looks by changing out one piece, like a skirt or blouse, from each. If there's anything you should overpack, it's socks and underwear, or layering tees and tanks. In winter, wear your coat and heavy boots onto the plane instead of using up valuable suitcase space. Finally, always throw in something small that can dress up an outfit (like a necklace or pair of high heels) and something to dress an outfit down (T-shirt or flats).

Next is the actual packing. Start with an empty suitcase and lay out one pair of pants with the waist by the wheel end and the legs draping over the suitcase edge. Repeat in the reverse with a second pair of pants. Next pack your heavier shoes (in little cotton bags, if you have them) toward the wheel end of the suitcase. For the rest of your clothes, fold each piece up the middle of the garment or along major seams to minimize wrinkles later on. Now fill in any "holes" with socks or underwear as a buffer. Add your toiletry kit and end by folding the legs of your two pairs of pants over your other clothing. I like to store anything that could potentially leak in double plastic bags (one zip-top and one grocery store plastic bag) in an external pocket. Always pack your jewelry or anything that could snag in a separate pouch or container.

Finally, make sure to pack a change of clothes (or at least a fresh T-shirt and a pair of socks and undies) in your carry-on just in case there's a delay in receiving your luggage once you arrive at your destination.

Fall

MIX AND MATCH, LAY ON THE LAYERS, AND COZY UP FOR AWESOME AUTUMN ENSEMBLES

Fall is my favorite season, especially when it comes to getting dressed. And although I've been out of high school for a decade, I still love the back-to-school shopping rituals I had with my mother as a teenager.

At the end of each summer, I'd start with a budget for my school clothes. At the time I thought it was massive, but looking back I realize that figure included a winter coat, boots, dress shoes, and Sunday's best within a pretty tight dollar amount. My first task was to go to the mall and preshop—I'd create a long list of items I liked along with prices. From there I'd decide what made the most sense from both practical and cost perspectives and edit down my list.

Next, my mom and I would set a date and *get shopping*! We'd go through the list, checking things off, finding new bargains, and making substitutions. And when I had a vision of an item that I couldn't find or that wasn't in my price range, I'd head over to the fabric store with my mom for material to make skirts and dresses. So much of my love for fashion and clothing comes from those mother-daughter design collaborations over bolts of fabric and pattern books.

Once at home, we'd lay everything out on the living room floor in head-to-toe-styled outfits. We'd step back and look at them for a few minutes, then pick them up and rearrange them all over again.

⊙ Fall: Pull from Your Closet

Mid- to late September is when I like to get my fall closet in gear using a mix of my year-round basics (black blazer, dark denim, black skirts) and warmer seasonal basics like a black turtleneck and thick cardigan. Pull your heavier-weight basics from storage as your starting point for your fall closet.

✔ CHECKLIST

- White or off-white blouse
- White or off-white layering blouse
- Dark turtleneck
- Dark blazer or jacket
- Cardigan
- Weekend jacket
- Dark winter coat
- Neutral dress

- Little black dress
- Printed black dress
- Weekend jeans
- Tailored denim
- Dark work trousers
- Dark short skirt
- Dark pencil skirt
- Dark full skirt

Fall Add-Ons

By now you've learned that each season you'll be pulling clothes from last year's closet, integrating transition items and injecting some fresh colors and styles into your wardrobe. As with spring and summer, you'll stretch your wardrobe possibilities further if these colors not only work with your neutral core basics but with one another as well. I've laid out two color palettes that work well together, both based around the printed and pattern colors in the dresses. In the first color palette, I've opted for purple and mulberry along with a basic navy jacket, black skinny jeans, and charcoal winter-weight shorts. For the second palette, I've gone with warm and rich gold, burgundy, and camel brown.

✔ CHECKLIST

- Solid cardigans (grandpa, chunky, V-neck) in secondary colors

- Solid sweater in secondary color

- Dark jacket

- Printed tee

- Printed dress

- Denim (in new wash or silhouette)

- Solid blouse in secondary color

- Patterned skirt or shorts

- Sweaterdress

- Trousers (in different color from your basic pair)

- Printed blouse

⊙ Fall Splurges

From time to time you'll find a piece you're in love with but that isn't within your price range. As long as you have the majority of your wardrobe already covered, I think a splurge item can be really special and totally worth it if you plan to wear it often. A designer dress, a souvenir sweater from abroad, or a statement jacket are perfect splurges. Still not convinced? Flip ahead to "Food for Thought: Cost per Wear" on page 98 for why spending for lasting quality is a money-saving strategy in the long run.

designer wrap dress   souvenir sweater   extra winter coat   statement jacket

◉ *Fall Shoes and Boots*

Your choice in footwear has a lot to do with whether you spend your day sitting or standing (or somewhere in between). My starting point for fall shoes are a classic black pump, knee-high high-heeled boots, and flats, plus a canvas sneaker for weekends. If you already have those covered, add-on fun, special-occasion shoes; transition sandals; high-heeled booties; short flat boots; and equestrian-style flat boots.

✔ CHECKLIST

- Classic black pump
- Knee-high high-heel boots
- Flats
- Canvas sneaker
- Fun, special-occasion shoe

- Transition sandals
- High-heeled booties
- Short flat boots
- Equestrian-style flat boots

⊚ Fall Accessories

Whether or not you can afford to update and add-on a lot of new pieces to your fall wardrobe or splurge on one fabulous signature piece, you *can* make some updates through accessories. Pashmina-style scarves are a smart way to stay warm and pull together an entire outfit. I have both the pricier and cheapo variations. If you opt for a less expensive scarf, be sure to iron it and remove the labels. When shopping for your accessories, don't spend too much on any individual piece, instead head to thrift stores and mass-market retailers for great prices on scarves, belts, and costume jewelry.

metallic belt

vintage gold broach

dark-colored pashmina

statement necklaces

wide neutral belt

watch

⊙ *Food for Thought: How to Shop Online*

I love shopping online—there aren't boundaries or geographical limitations of your local mall and it's great for comparison-shopping. Yet a lot of women are hesitant to buy without seeing, touching, and trying on in person. Keep these tips in mind to make online shopping a little easier:

- Measure yourself with the help of a trusted friend. Remember that your bust and hip measurements are taken at the fullest parts of your body and your waist at the smallest (not where you wear your jeans). It's helpful to repeat this process twice each year to ensure you order the proper size. Write these numbers down for the next step.
- Seamstresses always add-on what they call the *wearer's ease.* This is the extra space added to your body measurements that makes a garment movable and comfortable.

  BUST: add 2 to 3 inches
  WAIST: add .5 to 1 inch
  HIP: add 2 inches

- Now you're online and ready to shop. Always check the size chart, which can vary from brand to brand. You'll definitely want to work with your measurements (plus ease) instead of a "size." Most retailers will give the full circumference measurement, while vintage dealers use measurements taken flat. You'll need to double this number.
- Look for close-up photos of the fabric and stitch quality and

read the descriptions. Pay close attention to care instructions, fabric content, and potential for shrinkage.

- Have a look at the shipping rates. Some retailers will charge you shipping based on purchase price, not weight, and this can end up being super-pricey.
- Check out the return policy. You want to know what you're in for should you dislike the item or if it doesn't fit.

◉ Fall Work Outfits—Week One

For the first week of fall, I'll show you how to bring a little pop of color to your fall work wardrobe by utilizing your core closet in conjunction with your colorful add-on pieces and accessories. Let's take the old standby, the little black dress, and look at how you can make it stand out.

First, try some colored tights. For Outfit 2, I've paired hunter green tights with a printed black dress, blazer, and statement belt. There's definitely a playful vibe because of the tights, and that balances nicely against the seriousness of the blazer.

Next, transform a basic black sleeveless work dress by wearing a fall blouse from your add-ons *under* the dress. You'll want to choose a blouse that's not too voluminous or heavy, so it doesn't add extra bulk (Outfit 4).

◉ *Fall Work Outfits—Week Two*

> I've always suffered great stress over the dilemma of matching brown and black together. I can never tell when appropriate or not. Or does it matter at all?
>
> —Kiersten, 20, Texas

This week, let's tackle one of the questions I'm asked most often: black + brown = ?

Black and brown can absolutely be worn together! The key is to go with a camel or cognac shade of brown that slightly contrasts against black. You'll also want to make the match look purposeful (i.e., no brown shoes with an otherwise all black outfit).

A black turtleneck and brown trousers—two basic pieces—work together perfectly when accented with a big, bold statement necklace and a cuff bracelet (Outfit 5).

In Outfit 2, the majority of the outfit is black and white, but the little touch of golden brown on the jacket is an excellent example of how black and brown can be done properly.

◉ Fall Work Outfits—Week Three

Throughout this book, I've challenged you to look at your closet differently and to mix and match your clothes into new outfits. This week, let's check out a few ways to get more mileage out of your accessories.

One of my favorite wardrobe tricks is to use broaches as fancy safety pins. In Outfit 1, I've used a broach to keep a buttonless sweater shut.

Scarves look great in your hair and around your neck, but they also look awesome as belts. The scarf shown in Outfit 4 worn *over* a blazer exaggerates an hourglass figure.

⊚ *Style Challenge: Creative Workplace*

I'm starting a career in the arts administration world and I have a pretty eclectic style. How much should I express my personality and how much should I keep traditional?

—Lauren, 22, Cincinnati

If you're lucky enough to work in a creative field and spend your days in a nontraditional workplace, you'll still want to have some structured and sophisticated pieces on hand (blazer or jacket, pencil skirt, great slacks, comfortable shoes) to mix up with fun, colorful, and artsy items.

Whenever you're starting a new job, avoid the temptation to buy a completely new wardrobe before your first day. I made this mistake before I moved to New York City full-time and bought the kind of corporate clothes I'd been exposed to at jobs in Indiana. I had a closet full of slacks and blouses, but my office was more of a dresses-and-jeans kind of place. Take a chance to see what your co-workers, and especially your boss, wear to work and factor that into your next shopping trip.

> **PRO TIP:** Whether you work in a creative field or something a little more traditional, make a pit stop at the gift shop next time you hit up an art museum. It's a great source for unique investment jewelry and scarves, as well as less expensive tote bags and umbrellas.

◉ Food for Thought: Fall Hosiery

Once the temperature drops below 60 degrees I break out my tights and hosiery. They're such an inexpensive way to change the look and feel of an outfit. Lace tights have an undeniable sexy vibe but can be work-appropriate when layered over thick opaque tights (I love black lace with burgundy or purple underneath). Sheer and opaque black tights are always welcome in the workplace for a finished look. Depending on your dress code, you may opt to save the ribbed, printed, and pattern tights for the weekend, but for a casual or creative office, they'll fit right it.

> **PRO TIP:** Avoid an uncomfortable fidgeting on your walk to work by pairing your hosiery with a half-slip under all of your dresses and skirts.

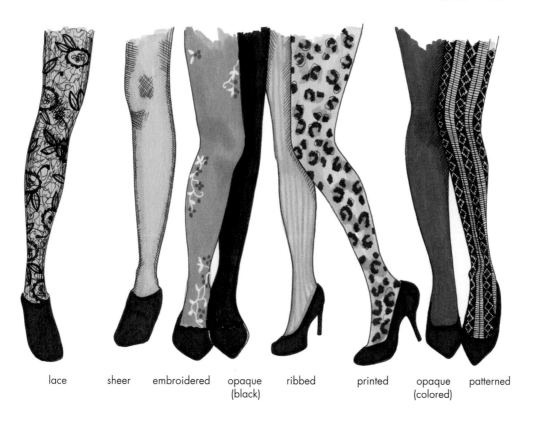

| lace | sheer | embroidered | opaque (black) | ribbed | printed | opaque (colored) | patterned |

⬤ Fall Weekend Outfits—Week One

I always feel an outfit is a little more put together when you use the rule of three—that is, make sure every outfit has at least three components (like jeans, a tee, and a cardigan; or skirt, blouse, and scarf). Here are some great ideas for weekend outfits that may even be appropriate for a casual workplace.

Keep your spring trench coat in your closet year-round. I like to throw mine on over a men's V-neck white tee with leggings and boots (and a fancy necklace) to look totally chic, while also being ridiculously comfortable (Outfit 1).

Just as I mentioned in spring, skirts don't need to be limited to work or a dress-up occasion. They also look great over the weekend. A cute printed T-shirt with dark (tights) and light (scarf) pinks make this basic black mini perfect for weekend shopping or brunch (Outfit 3).

⊙ *Fall Weekend Outfits—Week Two*

I do a lot of running around on the weekends, especially in the fall. My husband and I love riding our bikes to the farmer's market or taking a trip to our old neighborhood for brunch. Because I'm on the move so much, I like to layer shorts and short skirts over tights and pair 'em up with scarves, sweaters, and jackets.

When you're wearing tights under shorts, I actually think you can get away with a shorter length than what you'd wear with bare legs in the

spring or summer. In Outfit 5, gray shorts with slightly lighter gray tights look comfy and cozy.

The same theory applies to Outfit 3—I love this sweaterdress with nubby tights and a big, warm scarf around the neck.

⬤ Style Challenge: One Piece, Three Ways

A vintage printed blouse can look great for the office, the weekend, or an evening out. Here are three ways to get the most from a fall printed blouse.

dark printed button-up blouse

For the office, pick up on the golden brown color in the print of the blouse with a golden mustard-tone sweater. Keep the rest of your ensemble toned down in black (Outfit 1).

On the weekend, look cool and casual by pairing the blouse with a beat-up jean jacket, skinny black jeans, flat boots, and a cute hat and scarf combo. Leaving the shirt untucked adds to the relaxed vibes (Outfit 2).

Finally, if you're on the daring side, play with your patterns. Two drastically different stripes plus the delicate floral pattern of the blouse all work because they're in the same color tones. Black tights and shoes finish things off (Outfit 3).

⬤ Fall Evening Outfits

Rather than buy all new dresses for evening events, here you can see how some of your workweek and weekend closet can be remixed for happy hour or a nice dinner on the town.

Specifically, let's talk about bold-printed work dresses—I find myself buying these at a discount or at secondhand/vintage stores because I can't always tell how long I'm going to like them. But once you do track down a dress you love, be sure to visualize it as a dress, a blouse, *and* a skirt. A black skirt over this printed dress makes it hot to trot for a fancy night out (Outfit 3). How about throwing on a bright V-neck cashmere sweater over it and adding a belt with dark tights for the office? Or what about a tailored blazer or soft black cardigan? Don't get stuck wearing your dresses in the same old way each time! Mix it up and add a handful of *new* outfits to your closet.

Instead of wearing a sheer or mesh shell as a bottom layer, wear it over a camisole and layer on a fancy necklace, lacy tights, and a black-and-gold-striped skirt (Outfit 2).

◉ Food for Thought: Cost per Wear

When on a lean budget and building a wardrobe, a lot of women will opt for quantity over quality. I love thrift stores, off-price stores, and mass-merchant retailers for that purpose—getting a lot of trendy pieces on the cheap. But sometimes it makes more sense to spend more upfront, *what might seem a lot more,* to have an item that lasts for years. Introducing my *favorite* math equation:

Item cost / Times worn = Cost per wear

Here are a few great examples of items I've invested in for my closet:

FALL/WINTER BOOTS

All of my boots have lasted through multiple seasons—I have two pairs that have been to the cobbler and resoled twice each. They cost $200 and I bought them in consecutive years after college. Trust me, they were about the only things I bought those seasons, but by now they've ended up costing $0.25 each time I wear them. That's a good deal!

- For durability, go with real leather
- Take your boots to be resoled and polished each season
- Store them carefully
- Average wear: three times a week from September to March

LITTLE BLACK DRESS

- To make the most of this dress, opt for a sleeveless scoop or V-neck that hits at the knee. It will work for almost any occasion!
- Average wear: eight times a year for three years

QUALITY DENIM

I'm a jeans-and-T-shirt kind of gal at least two or three days a week. If you're also the kind of woman that wears denim day in, day out (and especially if jeans are OK in your workplace), you should spend a little more for some extra quality.

- Look for a dark wash and a leg opening that will work with heels or tucked into boots.
- Consider buying two pairs of your favorite style and having them hemmed to two different lengths to wear with higher heels and with flats.
- Average wear: two to five times per week

⊙ Storage: Shoes and Boots

You've probably seen massive celebrity closets with shelves and shelves and rows and rows of shoes—all cleverly organized by style and color. No matter how much space (or how many shoes) you have, you can organize your collection in an appealing and functional way.

Store your out-of-season shoes in their original boxes or stackable plastic boxes. I utilize the hard-to-reach top shelf of my closet for this purpose. If it helps you to stay organized, label the box or tape a photo (or drawing!) on the front.

For in-season shoes, I actually use a desk organization shelf that gives me three levels of storage. I keep this on the bottom of my closet and line shoes up by color and height. There's nothing more discouraging than a pile of mismatched shoes lurking in the depths of your closet. Keep them in their pairs and in a straight row. If you have a swinging closet door instead of the sliding kind, an over-the-door shoe rack works just as well.

PRO TIP: To store boots, I use a cheap and easy storage solution: reuse empty wine bottles or rolled magazines and insert them into your boots to keep them standing upright.

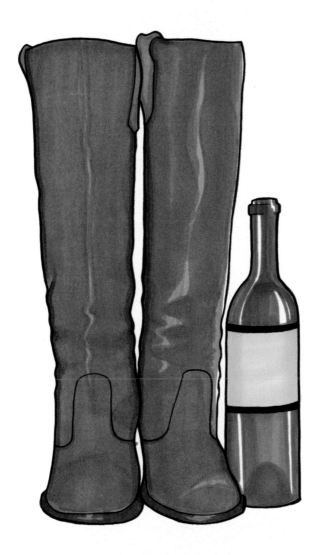

Winter

WARM, PRACTICAL, AND PROFESSIONAL LOOKS
FOR SNOWSTORMS, GLOOMY SKIES, AND
FREEZING TEMPERATURES

A lot of people don't love winter. I'm not sure I love it either (at least from a sartorial perspective), but I always look forward to certain parts of it, like my birthday (which is the very first day of winter), drinking hot cocoa by the fire, bundling up and running around outside like a kid after the first big snow, and of course the holiday season. There's always an event around the corner to look forward to in the winter months, but style-wise, it can be a little tough.

So if there's any time of year to let clothes cheer you up, this is it. Your winter closet should be comfy, cozy, and full of pick-me-up color but styled in a super-simple way. Maybe you have a short stack of neutral turtlenecks and cardigans that you mix with bold and bright skirts and tights. Or perhaps it's a selection of great trousers that work with a rainbow of fuzzy sweaters. One thing's for sure, just because it's inclement outside doesn't mean you need to limit your wardrobe to parkas and ski boots.

Work on your winter wardrobe and I promise you, getting up on a dark morning won't be nearly as bad when you've got a great outfit planned out. In this chapter I've got some great ideas for ensembles based around creative layering, new color combinations, and bold prints to keep you free and clear of the winter blues.

 Winter: Pull from Your Closet

The basic stock of your winter closet is very similar to that of fall with the addition of a few extra long-sleeved blouses and some darker, heavier layering pieces.

✓ CHECKLIST

- Dark V-neck sweater
- Light-colored blouse
- Dark cardigan
- Dark printed/patterned blouse

- Dark skirts
- Pattern skirt
- Winter white skirt or sweater-dress

⊞ *Winter Add-Ons*

For winter, look for a mix of thick and cozy sweaters and skirts along with some brighter pieces to transition onward into spring. Instead of two distinct new palettes, add-on pieces to round out your fall secondary palette.

✓ CHECKLIST

- Solid sweater(s) in secondary color(s)

- Solid cardigan in secondary color

- Funky hoodie

- Patterned sweater(s)

- Solid dress in secondary color

- Printed skirt

- Plaid skirt(s)

- Printed dress(es)

⊙ *Winter Splurges: Coats*

In the fall chapter we talked about "cost per wear" and how it can be better to spend upfront instead of constantly replacing worn-out lower-quality pieces. Winter coats are another excellent use of that philosophy. If you live in a harsh climate or you know you're in for a particularly cold winter, it's worth it to buy a coat with the extra bells and whistles versus just getting something cute and cheap—anyone who has experienced subzero windchills will agree with me on this one! A day-in, day-out coat that's in your core color palette should be your starting point. A well-made overcoat should last at least three to four years with normal wear. After you've covered your primary needs, a fun coat for evenings or weekends or in a different color is well worth the splurge. Sales start as early as January, which is just about when you'll be getting sick of your everyday coat.

military coat

vintage faux
leopard coat

camel hair coat

⊞ Winter Shoes and Boots

The majority of your fall shoes will carry over into your winter closet. Depending on your climate, add a pair of snow boots to the mix or continue to use your rain boots from spring and summer on slushy days.

I really recommend changing shoes at work when the winter weather is snowy or wet. Wearing stilettos on ice can be really dangerous and the road salt will ruin your shoes. I hate to admit it, but I throw fashion out the window when a blizzard rolls through town—you should, too.

⊞ Winter Accessories

Your winter hat, scarf, and gloves are great final touches to a completely pulled together outfit. I like to keep a basket in my coat closet full of winter accessories and change them up depending on my outfit and the fore-

cast. Knit and crocheted hats and scarves generally look a little more casual, while felt berets and floppy hats have a quiet sophistication. I like
loosely fitted winter hats because there's less of a risk for hat hair. My
curly-haired friends have told me berets are also excellent for not smash-
ing their bouncy locks.

PRO TIP: Think of your coat, hat, scarves, and gloves as an additional outfit. There's no need to be completely matchy matchy, but
there should be some coordination.

⊞ *Winter Work Outfits—Week One*

As I mentioned at the opening of this chapter, winter is all about finding
a look that works for you and your schedule (and climate), and this workweek is a perfect example. If you're more comfortable in slacks, invest in
a great pair that can work with a variety of cardigans and blouses, like in
Outfit 1. If dresses are more your speed, look for colors and prints that

can work alone (Outfit 2) or layered underneath a jacket (Outfit 3) or blazer. For ensembles based around a printed dress or skirt, you can take the versatility even further by changing up your choice in hosiery. Outfit 4 works as shown with matching tights but would also be great with black or violet.

⊙ Winter Work Outfits—Week Two

> I seem to have a great wardrobe until February, when I get sick of everything. Any tips to keep the winter blues away but still stay warm with tons of snow and freezing temps?
> —Sara, 26, Minneapolis

To keep things interesting in my closet, I not only have my go-to outfits, but also my go-to tricks to take those ensembles to the next level. Here are workweek ideas to keep you out of a winter rut.

- Outfit 1: Go all out and combine pattern (the tie of the blouse), texture (the skirt), and color (tights). The combination may seem wild, but it really works when you keep your color palette to two or three colors.
- Outfit 2: For a baby step into the world of pattern play, choose two pieces in the same color story with a similar motif but different layout/pattern. Pin dots and polka dots in black and white look surprisingly chic with dark burgundy tights. (Technically speaking, pin dots *are* polka dots, they're just super small, like an eighth of an inch or less.)
- Outfit 3: Shift up your shape by working a dramatic silhouette (like big bishop sleeves or a peplum) into your outfit. This sweater takes a standard black outfit to a whole new level.
- Outfit 4: Wear a happy color. OK, that definitely sounds sort of cheesy, but if you're a woman who lets the weather affect her mood (I am!), then a bright, cheery shade of yellow just might make your day better than an old black or navy standby would.
- Outfit 5: When you really want to feel pulled together, start with one piece from your closet (like a darling and daring printed

skirt) and add something loud (fire engine red tights and booties) and something neutral (collared lace blouse). The texture of the top and color connection of the leg-wear are different in tone but totally work with this wild skirt.

⊚ *Winter Work Outfits—Week Three*

For our third week of winter outfit inspiration, it's all about how to incorporate some of your vintage-store finds into modern looks.

Plaid wool skirts from the seventies are an awesome addition to your winter closet. Instead of pairing with other vintage pieces, create a more fashion-forward look by pairing with up-to-date basics. A basic black cardigan with flat black boots are the perfect match for this very retro bias-cut, buffalo plaid skirt (Outfit 2).

Another way to bring a vintage piece into the twenty-first century is to pair it with bold, colorful accessories like tights and gloves (Outfit 1).

⊙ Food for Thought: An Exception to the Rule

Although I'm a huge fan of injecting a dash of color into (almost) every outfit, I'll make an exception for black, white, and gray. I'm crazy about their versatility, especially when they're all mixed together like in this week's worth of outfit ideas. When you're working with a desaturated

color palette, go a little further with mixing up prints, patterns, and textures—like an oversized herringbone textured pencil skirt with crocheted black tights (Outfit 4) or floral lace tights with a polka dot blouse (Outfit 3).

⊞ Style Challenge: Valentine's Day

When it comes to getting dressed for a romantic date, take into consideration the type of restaurant/event you're going to along with the length of your relationship.

If you've just started to date a new person, less (skin) is more. Feel free to bare one of your best features (legs, arms, collarbones) but leave the back-baring and cleavage-revealing tops at home until you've gotten to know each other better (Outfit 1). There's nothing worse than being on a date with someone who doesn't look you in the eye because he's staring elsewhere.

Once you've been together a handful of months and are in an established relationship, there's more room to play with flirty elements such as flutter sleeves or a deep V neckline (Outfit 2).

For the woman in a long-term committed relationship, use this fancy date as an opportunity to really get dressed up. This one is just as much about you feeling sexy as it is being all done up for your date. You'll both appreciate getting out of your everyday routine. A confident woman is a sexy woman, so feel free to show off a little more skin, rock an up 'do, or try out a towering pair of super-hot heels (Outfit 3).

⊛ Storage: Hosiery and Accessories

By now you've amassed quite a collection of tights, scarves, belts, and hats. Here's how to keep them all organized.

To store hosiery, use a plastic hanger and tie tights in a gentle slip knot. Start by holding the tights at the toes and the waist and fold in half. Lay halfway over the bottom of the hanger and pull the toes through the loop. Organize by color and hang with your skirts and dresses.

For belts and scarves, I use the same clear plastic boxes I store my off-season shoes in. Store scarves by color and folded flat (avoid the temptation to throw them back in the box tightly knotted). Belts should be rolled and stored flat with similar colors (I divide my belts by black/brown and other). You might only have a couple of scarves and a couple of belts, but

by giving them individual storage space in your closet, you'll eliminate the risk of them sneaking off on their own (which always seems to happen to me when I don't put something away).

Last, hat storage. The way in which you store your hats will depend on the type of hat you have (blocked versus flat). Flat hats are berets and crocheted or knitted winter hats. Go ahead and store these in a clear plastic box. Blocked hats (such as floppy felt or straw hats, fedoras, or cloches) should be hung up on the wall, stored in a hat box (these are available in craft stores), or displayed on a wig form.

⊟ *Winter Weekend Outfits—Week One*

While at least eighty percent of your closet should work for mixing and matching, you should still have a handful of statement pieces for each season. For some women that might be an extra bright color; for others it's a strong print or pattern.

However, just because a sweater or jacket makes a statement doesn't mean you should limit it to only one or two outfits. This splurge jacket from fall (Outfit 5) works in so many ways because although the stripes are bold, the tan, black, and winter white work with almost all of the fall and winter closet neutrals. I love how an untucked blouse automatically looks easy and casual with jeans (but would also work for the office, tucked in and with black trousers).

Another bold pattern I'm a huge fan of is leopard print. Color-wise, think of it as a neutral part of your closet—it can look great with a solid black or bright color, like these rain boots (Outfit 3).

◉ *Winter Weekend Outfits—Week Two*

This series of weekend looks is designed to get you out of your mid-winter weekend rut! If you constantly feel like you pull out the same old tired jeans and hoodies, then it's time for an update. Even your casual clothes should make you look and feel good about yourself.

Start small by replacing your standard heather gray pullover sweat-shirts with something a little more fashion-forward, such as a flutter sleeve fleece sweatshirt (Outfit 2), embroidered cardigan (Outfit 3), or vintage sweater (Outfit 4). By tossing or donating your rut-inducing standbys, you'll be less tempted to fall on old style routines that got you to *blah* in the first place.

Also, think about wearing your winter accessories differently. A light-weight Pashmina-style scarf can enhance an ensemble both indoors and out (Outfit 1, Outfit 5). I actually wear my black Pashmina year-round—it's perfect as a hood in place of a winter hat and works equally well as an elegant shawl over a semiformal dress.

⊙ Style Challenge: Winter Sports Fan

When it comes to sporting events, I'm more of a casual/fair-weather fan than a die-hard fanatic. I like watching the big games on TV and occasionally going to the arena to watch in person, but I don't have a drawer full of team jerseys. So when the Superbowl or March Madness rolls around, I need to be creative in pulling together a sporty look with a touch of team spirit. Here are a few fun ways to get in the game:

1. Raid your closet for something near the team colors. You don't need to match exactly. A dark plum instead of bright purple still gets the point across. Same goes with rust instead of orange and navy instead of cobalt blue.

2. Go neutral and throw on a dash of team spirit—like a button. Yes! Buttons do still exist and are an easy way to update a sport ensemble of a funky hoodie, leggings, and canvas sneakers.

3. If you have a team T-shirt, wear it under a blazer for a smart, pulled-together outfit (which works well when going from the office directly to the sports bar).

4. Go for a vintage tee in your teams colors—even if it's not your actual team. An old tee-ball T-shirt in cream and crimson? Go for it! Have an old high school track T-shirt that happens to be black and gold? It works!

◉ Winter Evening and Holiday Outfits

I've always been the kind of girl who really enjoys dressing up, and that's just one of the many reasons I love the winter holiday season. I'm going to be mixing up your fall and winter closet with a handful of new go-to glam pieces to have you feeling festive from Thanksgiving to New Year's Eve.

Although the majority of your November and December budget probably goes toward gifts for others, don't forget to tuck away a bit of spending money for a few glitzy and glamorous seasonal items. For gals on a tight budget, pair up a new necklace or pair of sexy tights with one of your classic standby dresses. Or if this year marks a superspecial holiday occasion, go all-out for a new cocktail dress.

OFFICE HOLIDAY PARTY

One of my favorite parts of working in the corporate world was our yearly holiday party. Toward the end of the workday, we'd all trade our Secret Santa gifts before heading to a restaurant downtown. Like family celebrations, each office is different, but here I've suggested outfits that could work for your day at the desk and then easily transition to an off-site party.

A quick change of jewelry, hosiery, and shoes can make all the difference when you're headed to an event straight from your cubicle. I like to sass up a basic green dress with patterned tights and a big, glossy necklace (Outfit 2).

PRO TIP: Just as with summer work-related events, remember to keep your office holiday party choices tasteful (skip cleavage and back-baring tops).

HOLIDAY ON THE TOWN

For holiday parties out on the town (or really any Friday or Saturday night in December), go with a little more glitz than normal. I like to mix in some of my standby work/weekend favorites like a short black skirt or black blazer with sequins or shiny pieces.

Sequin leggings are a fun alternative to jeans and look awesome with a longer tunic or top—or even under a black dress with ankle booties—(Outfit 2).

I also love checking out thrift stores for sparkly sweaters. Usually in the boutique section and almost always from the 1980s, look for ultralow prices and high shine. I found this cream sequin sweater at a one-dollar driveway sale in L.A.! One of the best bargains of all time (Outfit 1).

PRO TIP: Limit your look to one or two pieces of shine (sequins, satin, jewelry, or lip gloss) and go matte for the rest of your outfit.

NEW YEAR'S EVE

If there's any night of the year (other than Halloween) that you can dress up as wild as you like, it has to be New Year's Eve. Because it's usually pretty cold in NYC, I usually plan my outfit around my transportation or plans for the night—if I've got a ride to and from a party (or it's at home), I'll go for a short cocktail dress and sexy high-heeled sandals (Outfit 1).

On the other hand, if I know I'll be taking the subway or hopping between bars, I'll wear a fun coat, tights, and walkable shoes (Outfit 4).

Final Words

I hope I've shown you that getting dressed is no different from following a recipe. Analyze your closet and wear something that makes you feel like a million bucks. And then you do it again the next day. And the day after that. Soon you'll realize you're having a really great year. Chances are it's not just how you look but more how you *feel* when you look good. For me, dressing in the morning in a really great outfit puts me ahead of the curve. It's why we feel confident in interview suits or ready to take on the world in our lucky pair of heels. It's a little extra dash of "can do" confidence.

Whether you're a college graduate who's building her first professional wardrobe or a woman updating her old favorites, I encourage you to build off the recipes I've shown you here and to create your own. My mom has a favorite saying (I apply it to every aspect of my life) that works equally well in the kitchen and in your closet:

Good, better, best
Never let it rest
Until the good is the better
And the better is the best

Acknowledgments

Thank you.

To my amazing husband, Adam Quirk, for giving me the blank sketchbook that would become *What I Wore*, for listening to all my concerns and reading through each revision of the book, for taking my daily outfit photo (almost) every day, and for his unending love and support. I couldn't have done this without you.

To my family: My parents and siblings (Dan, Jr. and Rebecca), I love you so much.

To my agent, Deborah Schneider, who saw the potential in my ideas and helped them grow.

To the team at Random House: Jane von Mehren, Jill Schwartzman, Liz Cosgrove, and especially my editor, Kerri Buckley, who helped take this book from good to better to the best.

To my friend Erin Loechner for being a breath of fresh air, a tireless listener, and an inspiring writer.

To my friend Rich Tong for giving me the job that served as my stepping stone into becoming a full-time blogger, for always being so excited to see my new illustrations, and for his feedback on the early versions of this book.

To tumblr for providing an awesome platform and starting a great community around it, to Tricia Royal for starting wardrobe_remix, to my peers—fashion bloggers who continually raise the bar—and to my readers for all of their encouragement and kind words.

About the Author

JESSICA QUIRK is the blogger behind What I Wore, a personal-style and fashion-based blog. Since 2008, Jessica has been posting photos and descriptions of her ensembles along with wardrobe advice, do-it-yourself project ideas, and behind-the-scenes peeks of the New York fashion scene. She has been quoted in *Women's Wear Daily* and featured in the *New York Post, Time Out New York, Lucky* magazine, and *Paper* magazine. Jessica has twice been a featured speaker at the Independent Fashion Blogger's Evolving Influence Conference during New York Fashion Week.

whatIwore.tumblr.com